ABOUT *A GLYPHIC HOUSE*

"Beau Beausoleil's poetry combines moral ferocity with a jewel-maker's precision and economy: meaning is hewn from the elemental, from sky and soil and quotidian debris, and we are left with incantatory traces of what is most quintessential and elusive. For me, reading Beausoleil can be like reading the footnotes to my dreams..."

—Michael Koch, Poet, Author of *Street Theology*

"I need Beau's poems in both my waking and dreaming lives. His narrow spare poems capture elusive thoughts and touch on subtle feelings. And these poems don't shy from the tough stuff, they register complicated responses to the political issues of our times. Beau is a master of loss, witnessed alone and as we stand together."

—Felicia Rice, Letterpress Printer/Artist/ Publisher of
Moving Parts Press

"Beau Beausoleil's collected poems read like small towns on a road trip in a dream-washed country, traversing the terrain that is one poet's life: to blink is to miss them. But if you pass through slowly, eyes not averted, what you see will haunt you for days. These quiet, astonishing poems inspire a contemplative reverence for life in all its small miracles and shades of grief and regret.

—Matthew M. Monte, Poet, Author of
The Case for the Six-Sided Dream

ABOUT THE POET'S WORK

"...extraordinarily compact, concise, stark poems, with great clarity of line."

—Carl Rakosi

"Yes, very eloquent poems: eloquence and vividness at great depths; a good deal of courage involved."

—George Oppen

A Glyphic House:
New and Selected Poems 1976 – 2019

Beau Beausoleil

BLUE LIGHT PRESS ❖ 1ST WORLD PUBLISHING

1st WORLD
PUBLISHING

SAN FRANCISCO ❖ FAIRFIELD ❖ DELHI

A Glyphic House:
New and Selected Poems 1976 – 2019

Copyright ©2020 by Beau Beausoleil

BLUE LIGHT PRESS
www.bluelightpress.com
bluelightpress@aol.com

1ST WORLD PUBLISHING
PO Box 2211
Fairfield, IA 52556
www.1stworldpublishing.com

BOOK & COVER DESIGN
Melanie Gendron
melaniegendron999@gmail.com

COVER CONCEPT/ART/DESIGN
Andrea Hassiba

INTERIOR ILLUSTRATIONS
Andrea Hassiba

FIRST EDITION

ISBN: 978-1-4218-3643-0

Library of Congress Cataloging-in-Publication Data

Preface

This collection includes poems published over the last 43 years, and significant new work from a long-established writer who is still breaking new ground and producing breathtaking poems.

As a poet my job is to introduce the dead to one another: the work of a life-long poet is one of the themes running through these pages. *These days bleed through my tongue and pen.*

Another theme is that of light and darkness, and how close they are to each other: *the light is fatal to itself,* observes the poet, *the sun burns itself up for light, and it is only wonder that takes me past each darkness.*

There is a sense of loss and complicity (*we are both ruined cities carrying the fingerprints of the missing*) and of horrors that, once seen, we cannot unsee (*That woman cut from her skin That man turned out of his mind*).

"Beausoleil is a master of detail, finding emotional depth in everyday sights (the cracked asphalt wearing through the word STOP) and situations (in the line for stamps at the Post Office … I stand weeping for you).

On a walk to the bus stop the poet passes a group of girls with a jump-rope and sees that they are ancient storytellers never at rest. He admires their craft, their unselfconscious street-theatre: how much like writing poetry this is. The poet finds himself waiting for the beat that I could step into / the arc of moving words …

This is his great skill, to enter the arc of a moment and illuminate it with the unflinching light of his small poems of blood and salt."

—Ama Bolton, Poet/Artist, Publisher of Barley Books (UK)

Try to look. Just try and see.
— Charlotte Delbo

Spring: trees flying up to their birds.
— Paul Celan

for
Andrea

Table of Contents

From *Harness Of Bone* (2019) Barley Books Press

New Poems
(2019)

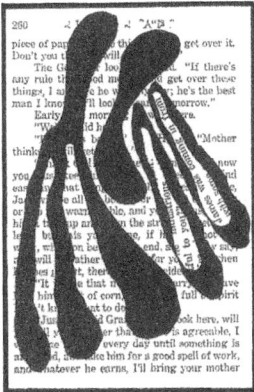

Untitled (March 15th 2019)

The trees
never stopped
remembering

they bent
without the wind

as each
of you
fell away
from us

Is there
any place
that is
a stronghold
of quiet

Is there
no way
to leave here
without anguish

At The Checkpoint

Show me
your hand
The one
you say
you can't write
another poem with

Now the
other one
that keeps
trembling
through the starless
night

Let me see
where you left off
reading

The line
and the page
that held back
the worst to come

until now

Hold your right eye
to every unwritten
erased word

carefully tell me
what you see

Cover
your left hand
and study once more
the invisible laws

Tell me
what you knew
from the moment
you started
to understand

 Lie down
 in the
quiet half-light
that collapses
between questions

After all
we are both
ruined cities
carrying
the fingerprints of the
missing

Then let us talk
in a hushed way
that rubs smooth
the roads
you have crossed

When did you
last sleep
without a fever

You may keep
 the keys
to the locks
that you will
never turn again

And the photographs
in your wallet
that I know you scatter
every morning
and later pick up

How many rooms
did you have to leave
to get here

Continue writing
your past
until you have
used up this paper

I already know your future

A Parable Of Working

The city
was first measured
in darkness

then light spilled
from the clouds
that had been sewn
above us

and people fell
out of shadows
into the open streets

The stars
appeared
to outline the way
to work

and to light
small apartments
above
corner grocery stores

And we heard first
our morning language
which had been resting
beneath the tongue
of our mother

Children
in the early light
saw how their parents
loved them
and each other

And they remembered
as they were
the day keepers

their skin already
outlined
with the lives
around them

The moon
had come
to help us rest
and now left
to comfort others

And there were
no borders
except for the corners
and the bus lines

Only memories
followed us
into traffic

Only the ragged wind
carried our hats
away

You See

I keep thinking
that this day
begins somewhere else

Maybe at that
crosswalk we
stopped at

the cracked asphalt
wearing through the word
STOP

Maybe behind
the lights of the trucks
driving the rain

Maybe under the
slow sugar
falling away into
the coffee cup

Maybe on the bus
as all the passengers
who missed their stops
turn around

Sometimes
I ask for mercy

I don't have
the right answers

That's why I'm here
with you
on this page

The Words

I want to
read to you

I want
the sullen light
to focus on this page

I want to leave
the locks unopened

I want to use
our pitiless knowledge
to break back in

And listen
outside the quiet rooms

In case we come home

Welcome

Work grinds
to a stop

 and we swallow hard
and leave it

What is left
of the light
changes
as we walk out

and we welcome that

And on the way home
we turn to one another
at each corner

crossing without safety
against the raging traffic

Every word that we know
continues to lose its direction

Every road that we pass is
going somewhere else
without us

We want
to open the last door
of the day
from the inside

We want
the dull ache
of sleep

to join us
back together

Driving Into The Central Valley

1.

We load the car
with a run of days

And the signs
we will need
to get off

and then back on
the highway

2.

Words move under words
as the radio plays
down along this earthen river

Every station that we
kneel at
plays for God and country

And the cities we pass
trade places with
the cities up ahead

3.

We both always speak first
and what we leave out

is about love

Which is as constant
as these fields

As constant as
the working lives
we only briefly glimpse

4.

And up against the mountains
that shadow each car
in turn

we pull over

And I cover your hand
with mine

Working At Night

I travel when
sleep occurs

my muscles knotted
like the neighborhoods
I cross to get here

I dream
outside my head

My night sweats
passing from block
to block
alongside the bus

I get off
and then back on
until I clearly see
my stop

I dream this night of my
left side

I dream of the
leaden winged angels

And the blues
I listen to

The blues
that never leave my body
even while I sleep

Walking To The Bus Stop

I pass
the jump rope
girls

who are flying above
the chalked
sidewalk

They are fierce
in their joy
of language
and motion

They are
ancient
storytellers
never at rest

Their jump ropes
crisscrossing in
the air between
their next line
and the sidewalk

love/marriage/envy/
betrayal / revenge/and stupidity
ongoing and remembered
forever in their rhymes

One sometimes two
or more
girls going about

their craft
in front of anyone
who stops to watch and listen

their dance expanding
into any cleared level space
they can find

I realize
how much like
writing poetry
this is

I remember once
being briefly allowed into
their company

And
then as now

waiting
for the beat
that I could
 step into

the arc
of moving
words and attention

that would let me enter
and stay inside

this ongoing song

Companions

As a poet my job
is to introduce
the dead to
one another

Sometimes
it's done in
a formal
setting

like a bookstore
or a quiet library

often
in a living room
with a carpet
and photographs
of family members
arranged around

Sometimes
it's more
informal

in a diner
or a parking lot

on a street corner
maybe at work
in school
in prison
or while
shopping

Sometimes
it's in a car
or next to a
car
sometimes
it's down
on the concrete
after
selling
loose cigarettes

Or creating
a disturbance
in civilization

Sometimes
it's done
in haste
as the person
falls
or is run over
or loses
their breath
to everyone
around them

Sometimes
I meet them
falling
down the
ocean water
as they were
trying to reach
somewhere

Sometimes
I come across
the missing
in a ditch
and I have
to pull them
out a little bit
so that
someone might
find them

And children

well

as you might
imagine
they are the
hardest
but also
the most
gentle

It was
always
that we would meet
where they
were happy

I would carry
them there

Be that
to their home
or alongside a

simple sidewalk
playground

But lately
its been
under bombed
out
buildings
or by their
desk
in a schoolroom

One
I remember
face down
in the water
with her arm
still around her
drowned father

one simply
washed
ashore
alone

at the demarcation
line

Sometimes
a loved one
reaches them
before I do

I offer everyone
I encounter

an extended hand
or embrace

a few words
of understanding

I found
my grandfather
once
by himself
in a winter field

waiting

He was tired
until he saw me
and then
called out his
mother's name

We see
who we need to see
to steady ourselves

I'm Here With The Muse

She won't
go into any
bar

that doesn't have
an unlit letter
in their sign

bad luck
to pass this
one up
she says

She wants her
numbers
to come up
right now
and so pretty

She wants to
see my words
drop down

like money
on the
table

in front
of her

Some nights
I can barely

stand upright
and listen

but she still
wants to
dance

She wants
to drive
a little
farther

a little
slower

She likes me
an awful lot

sometimes

And when
my lies
come into
view

in the
morning light
of the page

she closes
her eyes

and slaps me

This Half

Whatever hour
is taken
from harm

is on the spoon
that is closest
to your mouth

To have it
forced to
your lips

is to learn
the world
early

To chew
on the body
of bread

as you
fall

is to know
that when the
spirit entered
you

the first thing
it said
was

Try not to sleep
in this world

This Day On The Calendar

On this day
we are trying to gather
the lives and moments
that need illuminating

We need to remember
the women who
put their work down
on the factory floor

and walked out
to strike

We need to remember
the children
who were shot
in their classrooms

along with
their teachers

These two contradictory things
are part of remembering
on this calendar day

We mark this day
with small poems
of blood and salt

To help us remember
the ones
who were spit on

The one who were
dragged from
their cars

and beaten

Small poems of blood
and salt on this day

 to help us remember
those who were carried to
the rope

And those
who gathered there
and stood by
watching

as close as
my arm to
yours

or even
a hundred cities
away

We mark this day
with small poems of blood
and salt

shaped
with our hands

Poems that when taken

into our lives
make us unable
to swallow and forget

all the lies that have carried
us here

Verbatim

1.
I belong
to the
dogs

that
bark
up
the wrong
tree

on every
single
night

2.
I keep
my hands
where I
can see them

At all times

3.
Four
horses
came by

each with
a single
grace

their sweat
folded into
the running
night

4.

When
they
cut me
off

I turned
the shot glass
over
on the jack
of diamonds

and left
everything else
behind

5.

I could
ride
all night

and never
reach
the country
that left
me

We Are

What killed
you
was this
country

you only
saw it
at the
end

as it
rushed
up to
you

This big
wide open
country

I remember
you went
out
without
your hands
up

Each hour
hitting
at you
a little more

Until you were

freely
killed

like
the houses
torn apart
in the
flood plain

and before
today

you had
already
dry bled out
most of your
life

as we found
you

on the
sidewalk

or overdosed
on the
floor

And we stood
across the street
or up
against the
walls

observing
the closing
light

on the
highway

and in
the parking
lot

waiting
for your
body

in flesh
and
bone

to give
up

so we
could
carry you
home

and bury
you
inside
us

In the
cold

of this wide and open
country

When I Met You

I had
a child
with
notes and
numbers
in his
pockets

I had
a table
and a
chair

a spiral
notebook
of unwritten
poems

And a
bed
so narrow
we
had to
agree
to not fall
off

now
some days
I am
away from
you

alone
with poetry
broken
in my
head

And then
I find

some few words

and write
them down
on the ground

until they spell
your name

A String of Words

1.

There are minutes
in the morning

before I write down
where I am

when I want to start
for home

again

2.

I have learned
the words
that shatter
inside me

they no longer
wish to harm me

3.

A train is
lost on
a winter track

A string
of words
guides me

I beg the
distance
to bring you
into view

Suddenly Awake

1.

Memory
is so
abrupt

I know

you want
to be
singing

2.

I would
rather
look at you

than find
any open vein
of speech

on my body

3.

I am
my own
casualty

and lie down
in disarray

on this
open page

4.

Each night
staggers in

collapses
in front
of me

but some days

we want
to stop thinking
long before we sleep

On This Day

The night
settles back down
on the turning earth
without looking

We lower
our tiredness
to the ground
inside
a tight knot
of dreams

And far away
from here

some people
are alive
and not always dying
within arm's reach

In the morning
we will walk
through the
burning fields
of each
memory

and maybe pass
one of the days
that had been
set aside
for us to die

Then
we will cross
another measure
of open ground

only stopping when
someone close
has stepped out
of this journey

Then
we will either
pray or weep

even
as we continue walking

Along The Way

I read the names on
the reddened wall

I pressed each letter down
onto the tips of my fingers

I don't want to look
too far back

I don't want to see
the twisted wreckage
of days we left behind

I want us to feel
once more
a summer rain
approaching

I want us only
to keep moving

in this direction

Until everything
in our pockets
has a different name

My Daughter Celan

I wanted
to name you
after
the shadow
of one bird

I wanted
to stand here
with you

along this
stone path

and wait for
the moonlight
to fall

and break over us

In The Open

I was put down
to the ground

I was driven
down to my
knees

And even
in my soiled
bloodied clothes
I wanted only
to stand up
and go
home

to find
you again

as always

sleeping
in the warm afternoon

with an opened book
beside you

Two Questions

I have shed
all my dreams
of you
except this one

If I
start across
the sidewalk

to catch
the bus
that has arrived
from somewhere
else

If I stand
inside the
shelter

I will always
make something up
to catch your glance
before the bus
stops

Maybe a place where
the ground
rides above a city
empty of violence

or a rain
that waits

until it can
erase my steps
to where I am
now

I'd like so much
to talk to you
again

And if
one day I find
my way
home

If I cry
so hard
in the doorway

that you cry
and the children
wake up crying

will you
remember me
as I used to be

and take me
into the pattern
of your
blue skirt

Until then
I will wait
under this occasional
sky

under this single
hanging bulb of sun

And hope
to see you
in another dream

one that sheds only distance
and sorrow

Thc Wheels

The two halves
of the day
slow to a walk

but we take
no notice

The night tries
to find its way
out of the tight
blue sky

but we take
no notice

And we love
all the wrong kinds
of goodbyes

but we keep on
saying them

And when we are on
the last jump

there will be
one moment
still above us

At the
same time

on the
other side
of the road

someone
will be almost home

Cruel April

The moon
rents a room
down the hall

I only see one
side of him

He quietly slips
in and out
with a broken shard
of light

Some mornings
he is so pale

I think he
might be
junkie sick

Tears filling
his cratered face

I almost turn away

Any messages
for me
Anyone
still love me
he says
with that lopsided
little smile

Maybe next month
I say

Someone might call
or drop by

This is National Poetry Month
he says

And all I did for them
forgotten

Waiting

The best way
to talk to God
is through those
sleeping
on the bus

Be they drunk
or derelict
or coming home
from work
or shopping

so dead tired
that their bones
open easily
to heaven

Those who
sleep on
the bus
are the
swiftest
couriers
of prayers

I find myself
on the same bus
with them
on many
nights

and
write a
note

on the
rhythm of
the bus
starting
and stopping

turning my breath
at each corner

It is always
the same
note to
God

I write

These days
bleed
through
my tongue
and pen

I want to
risk
my faith
with you

I want to ask
only one thing

for you to stop
carrying
the torn bodies
of children
past me

Please
let this end

I don't seek
your blessing
or tears

or any easy way
out of here

My hands
are empty
and barren
as I write

Just let this end

An Empty Song

Deep in my blood
is the weight
of my childhood

An empty song
is everywhere

I talk it / sing it out
on the page
for you

later
I feel its quiet
as it slips back
under my skin

An empty song
that will not leave me

The texture of living
can rub thin

It's almost daylight
as the clouds gather

and I leave for sleep

We All Sit At The Table
Drinking

My mother
was maybe
seven years old
when they
took her picture
sitting
on a
saddled
pinto pony
on a
Bronx
street

She sits
quiet
in the photograph
in her
much loved
velveteen
dress

her small hands
clasping the
saddle horn

She is looking
past the camera
at herself
years later
from another
distance

I told her
that I need
to buy some
letters to myself

I need
to get lost
far away
wasted
on poetry

I need
to be
inside words
I said

I need to
watch them
bite and turn
like any other
animal

If I had started
riding then
she said
I'd be
somewhere else
by now

I look
at another
photograph
of her leaning
against my dad
as if he were

her tree
both grinning
in love

Everything has
broken down in my
poems
I said

And I seem
to like that

What you need
is a pony
she said

One that will carry
you
at seven years old

if one day
you have to ride away

From
Witness
(1976) Panjandrum Press

Blessing

Now sleep

Little bits of wax
over your eyes

The worst fish
raging in your mouth

Now wake
in reverse

Now hold
the place
of your body

recall
the strangers face

suffer this
and the flight
of birds above you

Now the real moon
is seen
And now
the Sun

Now the flight
of leaves

The trees
storm the brain

And then
you are the source
of all water

And then
you are the stone
that fills the ground
with light

Pursuit

No one
fire escapes you
no unimagined cloud
sentimental lover
step of a
dance
                of a family
no one sits through this
no one
feels the road ending
suddenly the car
your dreams
no one catches them
catches up
you ride
one hand
rolling down the window
your neck
shaking off its light

Turning

There are
certain dreams
on certain nights
that never happen

There are
combinations of numbers
that refuse to break up
and combinations
of words that become
deadfalls

There are certain dreams
on certain nights

There are things
you can't remember
because you have
become the memory

There are animals
you can't bring down
because you would
fall with them

There are dangers
you can't calculate

There are places
towards which
your arms reach
that would
hold you forever

Places on either side
that you have to
come back from

And there are the living
and the dead

And these too are combinations

Terms #3

I am anxious
and wild

It is your drifting
body

It is your
constant birth

All the pain
All the words

It is your hand
It is your moon

You the right eye
You the dog song

Without the sky
With only
the dark light

know me

I am here
for you

Jump against
my life

Crescent

The clouds
take up
the surface
of the light

Among the trees
there is suddenly
a clearing

And then your blood
is speaking to
your mouth

And then your mouth
is your companion

You give
your life
to this

You throw
away
your luck

The night
is all along
your skin

The path ahead
is lit
with darkness

City Night

One bone
now comes to rest
against another

This is one meal

The moon is played out

The clouds go back
inside the dead

This is one room

Now the street backs away
from the houses

Now the wind feels its way
to the corners

Under the haze
of electricity

Under all the individual
spots of blood

The cars
are jumping for it

The windows are
gathering glass

The night
breaks wide open

The stars
they lower down
until they are even
with our faces
then they slash
with their light

From
Five on the Western Edge
(1976) Momo's Press

Night Train

And when the night train
is coming in
filled with silver needles

And when the night train
is coming down
the vein of every track

And everything is pulled
after it
And everything is pulled up
and back

And when that happens
any number of
hard surfaces soften

And when that happens
there's no money
to sleep with
No money even to rub
the dust from

And when that happens
I cup my hands around
the dwarf star
of my heart

My hands cup below
the numbers that open
in my flesh

And the shadows
in my mouth
burst into fire

And the night train
comes up from the track
running its red light between us

And the night train is all
ivory white in the shade
of the moon

And when that happens
one of us is dead
and the other is in the
eye of the needle

And when that happens
we have paid for the
animal to die
And we have thrown out
a smooth rope for rescue

The Shark And The Swimmer

The shark and the swimmer
prepare for sleep

They lie on top of the water
their bodies shining against
each other like rough stars

The swimmer's brain
fills with smoke

The milk in the shark's
belly catches fire

They are farmer
and lover
in a quiet field

The farmer biting
his lover
just above the heart

The shark touches
the face of the swimmer

The swimmer joins
with the shark's body

They are dry fish
then red fish
then a tongue
that wakes and sleeps
with the same appetite for life

Thanksgiving

A storm
on the sun

A rolling away
of stars

Under this floor
it is beautiful
the shoulders of
this house crisscrossed
and strong boned

The house carrying
us quietly like
a knife in a pocket

The house aware
of the nails in the
honey of its wood

I play at lifting you
to the highest window

I ask you
what you see

I ask you what
you feel while your hair
twists out of its knots

I eclipse the light
with your body

This means nothing

The farmer putting
in another crop

The necks of some
wild turkeys snapping
on the concrete

The knuckles of
someone bleeding

The shooter putting in
another shell

This festive
time of year

This thanksgiving

Terms #2

The moon slides out
and after it
the bone slides out

The stars
stop in the dark
and arrange themselves

To love someone now
is to sail the ship
away in the bottle

To love someone now
is to understand how
the diamond is formed
under great pressure

See how it works

The night falls first
above the shadows

The heart slides out
and after it
the beast slides out

To love someone now
is to close one hand
and open the other

To love someone now
is to understand that
the sun burns itself up
for light

Passage

The light is liquid
The light is sacred

I want to bring down
the sun in perfect darkness

I want to see the blood
that runs its face

Once and for all

I want to carry the body
and kiss it

I want to untie
its knotted throat

A woman is crossing
a field in perfect darkness

She is carrying a bone
that brushes against the sky

Once and for all

The cars are crossing
the bridges like horses

The machines are
rubbing against our legs

The body goes down
in perfect darkness

The body is lowered to
a starting place

From
What Happens
(1978) Cloud Marauder Press

Passage # 3

No shade
No shadow

No bone
to raise up

The sun coming down
in darkness

The light broken
into stars

With darkness
the body
is trapped
in motion

With darkness
the word
goes after
the word

No reason
at the moment
of waking

The farthest night
will be this beautiful
and burning

Surrounding

The water
in the wave
takes its motion
from the heart

A bird
breaks with song

A line of flight
is ended

We think
that we have
seen it now

Every building
takes position

Every decision
ends in the night

We cannot pretend
that we see
when we have
seen enough

Every fence
reveals us

Every exchange
is not yet complete

We learn to move
in the street
so secretly

We discover
that what we want
from sleep
is not at all
what it has come to give us

Prepare

The wind
has come out
of its sleeve
of darkness

The sky's edge
sails toward
the unmade light

I build up
the fire
to equal
your fever

I look
to where
the moon
should be

Above us
the clouds
are beautifully
paralyzed

Around us
the night waits
to pass through
our sleep

Forecast

Add this
to the weather

The money
we have left

The money
we might get

Only the tide
comes in

The back roads
unravel
from the land

The back streets
twist into
other cities

Add the
unequal sleep

Add each life

the hours of work
with nothing to spare

Add each breath
that we lose

Each breath
that we settle on

Add what there is
of love

And these days
that are suddenly here
and then over

Add them full length
and the light and the rent
and the dark and the food

Add this
to the weather

Solitude

The highest part
of the tree
is constantly reborn
as the deepest root

The ground is
quarrelsome

This house sickens
it raises its barbed spine
and dies

I leave by the window
I am through with it

I return to myself,
arriving on some
unlikely night
waking my voice
with my body

I am
with well enough
alone

I will live
the river
until the river quits me

Lesson

Trying to pull
yourself back along
the words
trying to get close
to what holds
the flesh to them
So you talk
over the words
You shout
to the words
And the words
sometimes begin
just begin
to drag you along
like a bad leg
to carry you
to a place
where they can
turn and knife like
skin you
into other words
and move you closer
try to kill you
keep you there
or let you hear
however briefly
their deadly harmony

From
Red Light with Blue Sky
(1980) Matrix Press

Underworld

The thief
completes
the act of possessions

The one
who letters out the words

The one who carries out
the life

The one who sings
to find the level
of the door

The one whose song
is free of beauty

Now we have
the darkness

Now we have the dream
inside our coat

The value of waking
is its reversal

The light is fatal to itself

The Look

The fisherman
      fishes water

The genius
of the street
spots his man

A mistake
and you turn a circle
or turn maybe over

Maybe you hear later
hear it different

      One as one
      waiting around
      hit and gone

The bow of the boat
The number of the bus
The front belly
The wake of /
the hood of the car

And everything dead for combustion

Without Mentioning the Street

We push into the crowd
of the talking

stiff sweet heart
the breezes are leaving

The brick wall is fastened
And we gently bathe it

To show how it happened
she pulled in her hands

The trouble
she said
is not the worst
but you let it invade me

Unable to Proceed

Nothing is exactly
the mind

Shouting back
the body

Shouting each
color

The red
The money white

She said
Altogether
A person would like
to be escaped

She said
between us
we drink as much glass
as bottle

This to herself
she said

our image
a glyph / a
display of hazard

she said

            to
the sky

This is the double moment
of mistake and future

We are
nothing
but the mind is so
incredible
as to become
its own
necessity

Look Here

The signature
in the body cavity

The list
in the pocket

The sides
of the street
look like this

each eye
overlapping

That woman
cut from
her skin

That man
turned out
of his mind

That configuration
of change
at the bus stop

That release above and below

Consider the Root

The waitress shifts her weight
And looks at the ceiling

The cashier counts up
each overnight

The mechanic struck
the brain of the car

The mechanic got hurt

She explains
the motion
at the end
of her arm

She unwraps
the labor
from it

You shoot up a prayer
You buy from the menu

You lean over the sink
and feel for the water

Once my father
asked me
to believe him

I was ashamed
and beatified

I have not come any closer

Rocking

The cherry red dog licks
this certain sky

jumping
    Him
on the monkey
consider Her saying
deal them
liar please them
deliver
their machinery

The cataclysms
are in common

each brief
attention
bears
the outer day

and you find time there
your body is so bound between alchemies

From
Lascaux
(1982) Trike Press

The Painted Gallery

Is that your father
so violet
a red piece

so hunted
in common

between you
    a dance
that is separate
from its rhythm

Would you speak
if that gave you
no memory

      Your father
parting his legs

if that induced
no other death

between rooms
she leans against
the white wall

The woman giving blood
to his feet

Quick she is looking
at blood

thick bellied
in the orchard
of limestone

    jumps
the turned over ditch

the animal
twisted
and skidding
on the air of arrival

on his third leg

the track inside
the neck of
speech

      the light
blown into the eye

jumps
the body out

along the stem
of the brain

into the precise
uncertainty
that falls
up and down
the sidewalk

Which father
you know about

in you
which stays
underlying

On what terms

which promise
in question

in which motion
of despair

Which property of alarm
in the storehouse

A woman begins

searches the air
for its swarm of
dreams

follows her hand
inside the animal

feels
the light
contract
and then
widen

feels
the water
slowly climb
through the rock

she feels
the walking
of talking

walking outside
the border

do not mistake her

she is saying
                 not an embrace

saying to see there
              in the
              usual

the parallel hunt

where such walls curve
to contain

filling as they
    ready
their
    origin

saying blood
has passed
from her

has written
its slender stripe
across our back

followed
us into a
field of roads

tied us
in an ochre knot

entered
by its legs
the room

the contraction
of that beautiful
failed dialogue

From
in case this way / two things fell
(1982) Potes and Poets Press

Under Walking

The reading out
upon of motion
a letter

there the father

upraised other note
of sequence
only marked

even bird
attached
in place

explanations of work

several occasions
preceded in view
                raise a name

consider as quick
that invisible
expressive paralysis

that not one gone
stood his nerves
and still has mystery

Transformation

Now my sister
She can position

What grammar argues
to further happen

My father did

    So understand
what noun eliminates
that question

What will be moved

For Any Better

whether some
satisfy the next
word

really
that wound
is initial

     that lost
for things
looking

must see
that understand

having them live

Going Round

brought here
the birds arise from this leaving

once for these nights
we were rejoicing

they told
this singing

out there mother we are dressed

From
aleppo
(1984) Sombre Reptiles Press

meant for her

the length its after

and leave
they know the tables

it's their doorway
on the building

roaring over them

rigid bridge

permit my father
until one could

the countless recent
remember my brother exists

they came in the way
heated up

and many by now
were abandoned and undisturbed

at intervals
the family is served

have the same

perfectly gradually fear

what means
they carried the address

      /as they speak
the flat
the red part of the language

in this manner
are they drawn
through the city

pillow

the road stands in no refuge
riding is it both

which the fields obscured
and speech offers to this

the heaviest of ceilings
but we called the numbers up

held

since she numbers her hand

this gathers in
the personal

you lick it

especially the palm

the body
marks

the trucks
undergo nature

From
Has that Carrying
(1985) Jungle Garden Press

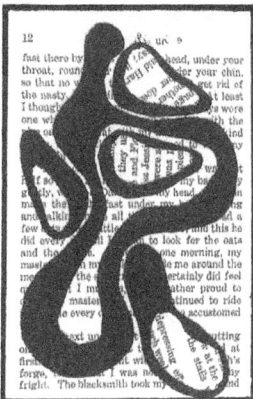

floating

the movies
beginning from

the true total
of working

ice-grey trees
each variety

the salty
juice

some looking

you see the nerve
on the bodies

how the
father sits

that up
at each night
our hands appeared
at the flanks
of horses

anyway, her teeth
to do the cutting

when it will imagine

dangerous blue
outside her

it's that minute

who even took
that luck
drifted that way

folding

the borders
are placed
in script

see-below
a lot of
town water

the little illustration
simple or plain

was when

the morning rotting
completely enough

some from the good
they been out

since now
the woman wrote

the lodger dressed

the sleeping
pushed upright

the window
seemed not true

not ready

From
Against the Brief Heavens
(2000) Philos Press

in the household

some one
spoke through

cursing everything
let's name

did all eat greater

nobody
without their
frightened portion

let's name you

well let's finally
name you

on the landscape

taken for the heart
and made empty

to the same example
did we deal for

as reading the capitals

the words
moving in their insulted knots

family

born in industry
ritual of ourselves

to keep sleep
to the law of desperation

several of several of us
working for the machine

in the late doorways

wounded of the
difficult world

icons of the open country

the question

morning
and evening

some man
stood begging

he called out
the customs
of the heart

as
these clumps
of salt

the scarred
and hesitant clouds

some man awakening
in the failure of thought

the trees
down in their
spiky forms

cherub

who faces
the man
into breathing

then what daughter
is dressed

the arm to the shoulder

what the day destroys
we who are known together

to be slaughtered
beside the recognizable

written

the visitors
drink at the table

they understand thought
to be realistic

the room is unimportant

From
Concealed in Language
(2002) Night Crane Press

a break in the trees

starting in the kitchen
uselessly listening to justice

there is a length of water
held in the breeze of heaven

a regret in the course of breathing
that makes two times the dead
the rule

surely time has ended among us

there is a break in the trees
everything falls to our inside

the habit of kisses

they photograph
as a brilliant misery
come to ground

as if some wandering light
had broken out of them

they are last standing
but rubbed with death

they have kept time
they have arrived at nothing

shoreline

my father
was turning
here

the sky
between
houses

to where
he walked

and looked

as though
he were

down
on the
ground

and its
murderous
speech

my daughter reminds me

some men drive
when the dark
has closed through them

they visit

they might be
carrying a coat

they are
a little apart
from disappearing

we have this in common

come to see

in the
room
that we
named
hell

she said
we are
not nameless

like birds
on the shadows

she turned
my wrists

there is
a kind
of rope
to speak

a circling
that we
leave
to listen

a fire
to the
west
of here

a texture
of light
on our
turning shoulders

our lady of the glyphic house

you told me once
how awful / and lovely
it was

and how little is firm
in our blue hearts

how this next forest
might happen to be calmer

with six less words in a row

From
Ways To Reach The Open Boat
(2012) Barley Books Press

Crossing

there are ways
to reach
the open boat

but each moment
is less certain

there are ways
through the ruins
of the tongue

but then one is stranded
in the visible

there are ways
to reach
the open boat

but I cannot contain
my memory

One

there are three words
at the wrist and the forehead

and these are the first words
of naming

there is a word in each word
a word responsible for the divine

and there are three words described of blood
and these are the words offended by memory

Four Crossing Dreams

1.

Out by the road
I wave to my daughter

We are both looking back

2.

Twice to the left
was water

And I beckoned to it

3.

My son is shaking
twelve dry peppers

he is whispering the words
that he needs to suffer

4.

I am angry with sudden hope

Your Standards

five trucks in a row
are an unmistakable
sign of cold days
and late nights

you understand loss
as a version of luck

as something exacting
under the lamp of
nightmare

people are often happy
in the summer

these are your standards

In The Bamboo Book — For Li Ho

pulling
pulling
the lines
into the
boat

scraping
the words
off
each fish
that has swum
ten thousand
li

pausing
to stare
at ourselves
without
reflection

Tumble

1.

that day the sky
was a paste of laundry

so I came early
and looked at nothing

2.

that night a storm
slipped across me

I wanted a question
from your unmovable lips

3.

an offer of that night
was for the field

just sell me some dirt
I said

just sell me some burning wood

From
Compass
(2016) Barley Books Press

Map

        I am listening
to your disappearance

I go back into the room
and turn the radio down

I have to cover each sentence as I read it

Her Mechanic

always a series
      of objects
    to be feared

 and always
a shout from the
other side of the door

     and in the car
we ache for what
we have just driven past

there is without end
the pain
of each thought
that continues

and haven't we been knocked
           around and around
                this room

and in truth
aren't we here
only talking
in sympathy with talking

Fallen

1.

Language is fixed
in my mind

it has its own
motionless melody

2.

This war
is bound to us
in our mortification

3.

These dossiers
must be stamped

before this table
has burned down

4.

How can we breathe
the blue sky
in this photograph

Wait Rose

on her way
to us
among the tables

she looks
to the side
of her skirt
for a spoon

water spills
and there are
occasions of music

she is
lost in the
voices

but has
in her wallet
a picture
of herself

while around her
the blood engine
of each mouth awakens

Compass

You said
bring me to that place

where we can sweep the words
into each corner

where we can sleep
as the blood dries over us

but I haven't seen you
since that day

and now is the third hour again
and tomorrow the third year

and my kitchen prayers are not easy
anymore

and it is only wonder
that takes me past each darkness

Where It Breaks

you might
be writing
against
what you
remember

or be
reading
on the
stairs

and after
each line
something
might look
the same
again

at least for a while

and I
wonder
who finds
your notes
that you
still leave
for the
missing

the ones
you write
on those

slips
of hard
paper

and in
the end

a tree
might
slide off
this page

and put
its roots
near you

alongside
the wild
onions

in this
green green
spring

From
The Long Distance
(2019) Moving Parts Press

like an incomplete breath

1.

I have
an image
of a way

to talk
to you

maybe
a way
to kiss
you

on the
underwing

2.

when I
was last
in your
memory

as we
walked

past
our bodies

I remembered
when those two sparrows flew between us

the long distance

I miss everything
he said

even those little girls
that we used to see
as they walked to school

even those
songs of suffering
that always played
on your radio

I am still lucky sometimes
she said

and last night
I dreamt a map
for you

use it

but remember
only follow the roads
that I alone
marked on your body

the fourth photograph

and apart
from you

I carried

our suitcase
that we
filled with winter

and apart
from you

I was
among the others
who were no longer passengers

but in the fourth photograph
we are together

and I am reaching for you

interior rights

1. you have the right
      to not remain silent

2. you have the right
      to understand

3. you have the right
      to infuse any present moment
      with social justice

4. you have the right
      to feel compassion and empathy
      for any people

5. you have the right
      to identify the unseen
      before it crushes all of us

6. you have the right
      to see inequality and cruelty

7. you have the right
      to forgive but never forget

8. you have the right
      to say, "this is unacceptable,
      it must stop now"

9. you have the right
      to remain Human

the lens

I brought
these wounds to you

which stitches
cannot close

that was my mistake

your death (for C.B.)

1.

I don't want
to reassemble

your anguish

as each day
comes this far
down

2.

I don't want to insult
your body
with any rolling memory

3.

and at the table
at dinner
even as the ground here
seems calm

I feel sometimes
the cold
alongside my words

inside my
throat

and I want to remember
everything
about you again

cut away from the day

1.

there
is a refugee
out in an open field

a raisin
in one of her closed hands

and far away from her
is a desk

2.

and here
we see this
through our windows

this reddish dark earth
is where we share
our happiness

where we lower
ourselves so as
not to see

another field

From
Harness Of Bone
(2019) Barley Books Press

Who Might We Ask

1.

There are some
streets in heaven

that are here
close by

but not seen
by someone

like myself

2.

Sometimes I look for
a plowed field
to walk through

the earth
turned over
in such a way

that I might
recognize some
root

of my
own memory

3.

There are
two trains

running this
one track

coming and going

but both
let me off

farther and
farther
away from you

4.

I look down again
into the standing water
in the shallow ditch

and see the clouds
above my shoulders

as they move
away from me

5.

I read in
the newspaper

of an
eight year old

in a refugee camp

who talked of
suicide

in a quiet ordinary voice

Held To This

A snake stops
and tells me
a story

Because he
remembers my father
as a child

A crow
pulls some clouds up and
over the border

I knew your father
he says / we shared
an eye for trees and dreams

And for the dead and who sits
with them / and after
who carries them
away

A field mouse
lies trembling
in my hand

You are not my ghost
I say

And put it down amidst
the wild grasses

And see my father

The Precise Moment

There
in the line
for stamps
at the Post Office

I suddenly
remember you
again

As you wash
over me

Drag me
under

As the pain
within each fragment
of that memory
comes together
inside me

Roughly holds me down
below the surface
of my own life

And at once
I stand weeping
for you / and then myself

While aware
that the others
have stepped away

Leaving me alone
but carefully watched

A Note

I want
to hold
a stone
to my
eye

so that
I can
see my
childhood

I want
to fall
down
hard

and not
come
to rest

I want
to walk
outside

and look
around

as everyone
puts their
guns down

into the
buried
earth

One Outside Three

I would
see him
some mornings
in the kitchen

looking as lost
as in
any family
photograph

He would be
holding hard
to his half-filled
coffee cup

as if it might
rescue him
when
the ship sank

or maybe hold him up
when he fell through
the thin ice
under his chair

I found
my own bad luck
he once said
to me

and now I can't
let it forget me

And then he
would go back
to staring out
at the backyard

trying to see
some work
he might do
out there

with just his hands

Where You Left Us

1.

I have not
learned the world

but instead
stand on part
of the sidewalk

and refuse
any help

in calling out
the words
of my lament

to anyone near

2.

Now
everyone
in the house
is weeping

roaming
from room
to room

alone
and in pairs
like wounded
birds

their arms
trying to
reach

back up into
the sky

away from here

About the Author

B eau Beausoleil is a poet and former bookseller based in San Francisco, California. He is the founder of Al-Mutanabbi Street Starts Here, a book arts response to the car-bombing of al-Mutanabbi Street (the street of the booksellers) in Baghdad, Iraq in 2007.

www.ingramcontent.com/pod-product-compliance
Lightning Source LLC
Chambersburg PA
CBHW031253090426
42742CB00007B/435